# NO OTHER WORD

*New and Selected Poems*

by

Barry McDonald

THE MATHESON TRUST
For the Study of Comparative Religion

© Barry McDonald, 2020


This first English edition published by

The Matheson Trust
PO Box 336
56 Gloucester Road
London SW7 4UB, UK

www.themathesontrust.org


ISBN: 978-1-908092-21-2

British Library Cataloguing-in-Publication Data.
A catalogue record for this book is
available from the British Library.


Typesetting, cover art and design by Susana Marín

# NO OTHER WORD

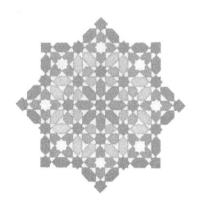

# CONTENTS

In Memory of Frithjof Schuon
*Infinite Gratitude*

"Say 'yes' to God, God will say 'yes' to thee;

This is to Heaven's gate the golden key.

About my earthly road I do not care;

It may be long; short is God's road to me."


∾


"O thou who seekest me, do never ask

Which is my homeland, nor what is my name;

The Universe is made of Light and Love,

And from this Light and from this Love I came."

—from *Road to the Heart* by Frithjof Schuon

For friends who travel in God

And, with eternal love, for Batinah

# PREFACE

P OETRY IS SACRED; consequently, the purpose of these poems is to affirm the Truth and Beauty of the Real, and to turn attention to the necessity for the remembrance of God:

> *The only story that does not deceive*
> *Is telling how the soul returns to God.*

> ∾

> *Under the witness of the rising sun*
> *One tale, holding all history, is true:*
> *The wisdom of the heart has always known*
> *From God to God the world is passing through.*

All who seek the Real are travelers on what Frithjof Schuon has termed 'The Road to the Heart'.

Composed according to canons of traditional prosody, the defining thought at the heart of this book is the Oneness and the Totality of God:

> *In consciousness of God our work is done*
> *Each thought leads from the many to the One.*

> ∾

> *No longer caught in time, its spell undone,*
> *And every thought returning to the One.*

These words echo the metaphysical vision of the saints and sages, That which is discerned by the vision of 'the eye of the heart' as the most enduring subject matter for poetry. Such poems should arise from the center of the soul; in that center resides the theomorphic

Substance, the Reality of who we are in God. In a distillation of si-
lence and word, we seek to realize an expression which is direct, clear,
exact, simple and harmonious; devoid of casual and conversational
speech. No straining for 'originality'; rather, repose in the Origin.
These are songs of spiritual wayfaring:

*Arriving where the soul and Spirit rhyme*
*Deep in the heart the bells of Heaven chime.*

~

*Why are they passing through the here-below?*
*To know the Truth, and be the Truth they know.*

Founded upon the defining ternary of the *Religio Perennis*—
Truth, Prayer and Virtue, this book is a meditation on metaphysical
Truth and the remembrance of God. In consciousness where 'Only
the Absolute is always new', these verses flow into a single voice, sing-
ing in praise of the all-encompassing Reality of the One.

# NO OTHER WORD

# NO OTHER WORD

Because the Truth is all that it may tell,
The heart unceasingly repeats *Allah*.
No other word will have the final say,
The fate of darkness is to fade away.

In silent cloisters of the here and now
Our freedom is perfected when we bow;
We shall let go of all that is not true,
In prayer we learn all we need to do.

The sun pours down its radiance of gold;
The beauty of the light does not grow old.
The heart illumined by God's Name reveals
No vision but the vision of the Real.

# THE POOR IN GOD

The poor in God are beacons of the age
And quiet words of prayer are all they own.
Through every state of soul they travel on—
The invocation is their pilgrimage.

What is there left for them to see or do?
They find their happiness while passing through.
The ego like a wave rolls on the sea,
But there is something deeper they would be:

A single voice, older than Abraham,
Weaves consciousness through flesh to say *I am*.

# THE SHORE

Although men say there is no Absolute,
The sun stands like a prophet in the sky.
Thinking the truth is that there is no Truth,
The mind sinks root into the deepest lie.

While shadows of opinion rule the night
A few souls on the shore of morning meet.
There God still sings Himself into the light
And from the heart of silence wise men speak—

And in the moment time is passing through
The oldest prayer remains forever new.

# THE VOW

Like rising stars that blossom in the night
The souls invoking God are steeped in light.
Their knowledge centers on one certainty:
*He is with you wherever you may be.*

The vow they made, taking the Master's hand,
Requires all that they are to understand
The whole they seek is found in every part.
Drinking a wine that's flowing from the heart

They touch the nakedness the Truth reveals,
Till emptied of themselves they taste the Real.

## THE OASIS

The true oasis in the soul's mirage;
It's there they learn what traveling is for.
The miracle of consciousness sees far
And in the heart they build a hermitage.

And as the flowers of Remembrance bloom
They wait in peace to blossom in the tomb.
What knowledge plunges them in deep delight?
What treasure buried in the ground of night?

They do not fear the fading tracks of time;
The Name of God makes earth and Heaven rhyme.

# THE ICON

The poor in God must learn to travel light;
A prayer is all they carry on the way.
Why fear the time that chips away at life
When from the here and now they never stray?

They see creation is by beauty lit:
The world's an icon of the Infinite.
All parts, in perfect equilibrium,
Reveal the Self-Disclosure of the Sum.

And since the Oneness of the Real holds claim
There's nothing that does not repeat God's Name.

# THE REFUGE

Say *la ilaha illa 'Llah* and find
The knowledge at the center of the mind.
More than a testament of piety,
These words are threads that weave Reality.


The refuge of the consciousness of God
Is where all travelers on the way are led.
And there the labor of this life is done
Till all they are submits before the One.


Let time erode the things their eyes can see—
A man who dies before he dies is free.
In all they know, affirming the Divine,
The Spirit through the soul begins to shine.

# THESE WORDS

Say *la ilaha illa 'Llah* and find
The diamond of Truth deep in the mind.
These Words, like *Mantra* and *Upanishad,*
Unveil the Wisdom from the Heart of God.

Invoking *Allah* underneath our breath,
This Word can liberate the soul at death.
No matter where we go in time and space,
No home is found except in God's Embrace.

# WINTER STARS

The Orison we carry to world's end
In every trial will be a constant friend.
We suffer dreams men write into the frost,
But calling on God's Name we're never lost.

Though *Kali-Yuga* darkens points of view,
What's false serves only to reveal the true;
And since there is no god but God alone,
And every road from God to God leads home

We watch the stars that rule the winter night;
Their message is the victory of light.

# THE TREASURE

Setting a ring-stone is a jeweler's work,
But wise men place the Truth in every word.
Not rubies nested in the finest gold,
Their treasure is the consciousness of God.

A midnight bell rings at the end of time,
But through the darkness wisdom is revealed.
A few wise men pass round a cup of wine,
And praise the naked beauty of the Real.

# NO OTHER ART

Our pride and passion, idols made of clay,
We here and now completely cast away;
Remembering the Real, no other art,
No fading dream disturbs a waking heart.

No longer caught in time, its spell undone,
And every thought returning to the One;
Ideas that do not help us transcend,
We leave them in the dust and say *amen*.

Absorbed in God, let ego's temple fall;
The naked man owns nothing but the All.

# THE WISE

Among men or alone on mountaintops
The wise live in the Presence of the King.
Because they see the deep nature of things,
Through them a stream of prayer never stops.

Down through the centuries in every place
The saints remember God both day and night.
Some of them are like eagles in full flight
And others leave the world without a trace.

But while they live they own a single theme:
In silence and in song they hear His Name.
In different words their message is the same—
Because the world is more than just a dream
Their certitude shines like the summer sun
And they see through the many to the One.

# INQUIRY

# INQUIRY

*Who am I* was the question of a sage;
The answer has been sought in every age.

While ego dreams, ideas rise and fall,
We sit and quietly invoke *Allah*.

The Truth we seek to be is not so far—
The Name Naming the Named is who we are.

# THE RETURN

Although we walk together down a road
We are like raindrops falling to the sea.
The world is never what it seems to be;
The only story that does not deceive
Is telling how the soul returns to God.

Some pilgrims travel to the holy land,
While others close their eyes and sit quite still.
The reason is not hard to understand:
All of creation tends toward the Real—
Even a speck of sand becomes a pearl.

Year after year the restless soul may search;
A plain and simple flower shows the way.
Blooming out of the darkness of the earth,
It turns its face toward the light to pray.

## SAY *ALLAH*

To all desires that echo in the mind,
And to the voices crying in the wind,
And to the web of whispers in our thought,
We say *Allah!* Then leave them to their talk.

Because on earth we have not long to stay
We seek the hidden kingdom of the heart.
We see and we believe deep in the dark
There is a star to guide us on our way.

# SANDCASTLES

Like sandcastles beside a rising sea
There are no worldly dreams that we may keep.
Death draws us near, as waking does to sleep,
What's nearest to the heart is all we seek.

Behind each veil discern the Absolute;
With every lesser treasure now be done.
With nothing but the beauty of the Truth,
A wise man will stand naked in the sun.

# LIKE SUNLIGHT

In this Eternal Moment, here and now,

Before the Absolute alone we bow.

With consciousness of God in every thought,

The soul by truth and beauty must be taught.


When death in life and life in death accord

We stand before the Presence of the Lord.

No specter of illusion may persist—

Death comes like sunlight burning through the mist.

## LIKE SUNLIT CLOUDS

Like sunlit clouds in time we fade away;
Our fate is woven by the words we pray.
With eyes of love and knowledge we discern
The necessary things we strive to learn.

Because God lends His Oneness to the world
Remembering His Name we never part;
With souls like weather-beaten sails unfurled,
Our compass needle points toward the heart.

# THE EAGLE

Because the human eye cannot see far
We pray to see things as they really are;
To rise up like an eagle soaring free,
To know and love the Truth we long to be.


And high above the valley of the soul
There is a world where time does not grow old—
No grief or laboring, no fearful night;
The dreamer wakes inside the eagle's flight.

# THE MIND

The mind's an eagle meant to rise and soar;
It cannot rest until it knows the Truth:
*No absolute except the Absolute—*
All other knowledge, by contrast, is poor.

To see things from on high and to fly free,
There is a beauty we must learn to be.
Beyond all thought of how or what or why,
The eagle's outspread wings embrace the sky.

# FOR THOMAS YELLOWTAIL
*Crow Medicine Man and Sun Dance Chief*


So high an eagle rises in the light
It disappears, and yet it is not gone.
Its wings outspread to vanish in the sun
And there are men who sing to know its flight:
*Nothing lives long except the earth and sky.*


Round campfires in the night the old men rest.
Their tipis softly lit; of victory
They sing with solemn voices high and free.
Each naked warrior is with glory dressed:
*Brave hearts there is no better day to die.*


And there are men who dance to ancient song,
While others drum and dream an eagle's cry.
The mountains turn under an eagle's eye,
And to that height all things on earth belong.

# THE ALCHEMY

Awakening in God, we live and die—
The here-below seen through an eagle's eye.

No matter what we suffer in this day,
Deep in the alchemy of Truth we pray;

And through each trial our destiny reveals
We praise the fate that brings us to the Real.

## ON FAR HORIZONS

In timeless Truth, primordial and free,

There is a wisdom we must learn to be.

On far horizons and within ourselves

We seek the signs of God, and nothing else.


In this Eternal Moment we pass through

With every breath creation is renewed;

And through each veil, affirming God alone,

We find a world where prayers are at home.


And while on pilgrim roads we travel far,

We find the Truth we seek is who we are.

## ALWAYS NEW

To rid ourselves of all that is not true
In stories of desire we cannot stay.
What better work on earth for us to do,
The road we follow is the Word we pray.

The world appears like a kaleidoscope—
In changing shapes and colors men find hope;
But all that's changing one day fades from view:
Only the Absolute is always new.

What is the meaning of this life on earth?
Without the One, what are the many worth?

# THE VINTAGE

# THE VINTAGE

In all we seek to be till life is done
Our purpose is to realize the One;
And as we travel through the here-below
Each thought is guided by the Truth we know.

The consciousness of God is flowing wine—
We drink until we leave all else behind.
Although the Vineyard is beyond our sight,
The Vintage fills each word of prayer with light.

## PRAYER

Though many roads into the world appear
No matter where we turn the Lord is near.
In all the passing hours of the day
Reality is where we kneel and pray.

Men dream their lives away, but here and now
A star descends into an empty soul—
Somewhere a solitary man bows down
And with one word turns darkness into gold.

## EDEN'S GOLD

Because Creator to creation flows
Deep in the day the gold of Eden glows.
The eye of certainty sees everywhere
God is as close as light is to the air.

In every tapestry that *Maya* weaves
Discern the Pattern every sage perceives.
Upon the sunlit earth where wise men kneel
Each flower is an altar of the Real.

# THE NECESSARY WORD

To send us strength to face our final end
*Allah* into a waking heart descends.
Through possibilities that weave the day
This necessary Word alone we pray.

Invoking God, we are completely free;
Let *Maya* dream, we fear not losing touch—
Like living icons we must learn to be
Not such and such a man, but man as such.

## TILL WE DEPART

Because in suffering the Lord draws near
Let light of love replace the flame of fear.

In facing death we keep these Words in view:
*Remember Me, I will remember you.*

While passing through this life, till we depart,
Let consciousness of God shine in the heart.

VIGIL


Men dream the shadow-play of history;

We live and die, together and alone.

The here-below is not our final home;

All men are born to face Eternity.


Why am I on this earth?  And should I fear?

Sit quietly, invoke the Name of God.

Stay vigilant, although the night draws near—

Repeat again the liberating Word.

## LIKE ANCIENT RIVERS

*Samsaric Maya* is a dream, a snare;
But we awaken in each word of prayer.
And we discern, remembering the Real,
In every dance of veils God is revealed.

Like ancient rivers winding to the sea
We flow into the deepest Mystery—
The soul, a quiet dove, rises above;
Its final home found in the Heart of Love.

# THE ROAD

A man alone out walking on the road
Begins and ends his journey with a step.
This moment, passing now, he knows the Word
Of God is closer than his deepest thought.

Over his head, through broken clouds, the sun
Shines on the road to lead the traveler home.
The here-below is more than just a dream;
Through every flower God wants to be known.

# NO DESTINATION

Like all the blessings that a lifetime brings
The snowflakes fall and purify the night.
A sandalwood stick burns, a candle sings,
A man in silence prays for love and light.

Outside a snowy path leads to the world—
There is no destination but the Name.
Because one man invokes the saving Word
There glows through darkness an eternal flame.

# REMEMBRANCE

As burning candles disappear in flame
And flame into the darkness disappears,
Resting in God, we have no other aim;
We travel to a death where He is near.

As echoes in a canyon fade away
We leave behind another passing day.
Within the silence of the evening light
We vanish in His Mercy and His Might.

From dreams of other journeys we depart;
Remembrance is returning to the heart.

# THE BELLS

To realize the heart's primordial norm
Opinion into Truth the wise transform.
Turning away from ambiguity,
They rest in what they know with certainty.

And as they walk into the morning light
The miracle of all that is burns bright—
The sun is pouring down to send its rays;
The carpet of the earth is where it prays.

Arriving where the soul and Spirit rhyme,
Deep in the heart the bells of Heaven chime.

# THE HIGHEST GROUND

*in memory of Martin Lings*

In this eleventh hour prophets warn,
Delusion threatens like a rising storm.
Now in the mind the devil spins a wheel;
Few wise men concentrate upon the Real.

We walk in prayer and quietly pass by—
Like ripples on a pool we cannot stay.
Why fear the shifting shadows of the day
When only in the dream of time we die?

In this brief life we seek to rise above,
To stand upon the highest ground of love.
Leaving behind all sorrow and discord,
The soul takes flight remembering the Lord.

# THE COMPASS

# THE COMPASS

Still as a boulder in a flowing stream
In solitude a man sits down to pray.
A life is shaped by all this moment means
And by it he is guided through the day.

On earth there is no better work than this:
To learn what's necessary is an art.
Rooted in Being, Consciousness and Bliss,
God's Name is the true compass of the heart.

# THE WORLD

While lovers in ecstatic moments dwell,
Ascetic monks keep vigil in their cells;
A sculptor touches clay, a face appears,
A soldier prays until the Lord draws near.

Cloud palaces that drift across the sky,
Their kingdoms vanish in a traveler's eye.
A man like others who have gone before,
A page is turned and he is seen no more.

Under the witness of the rising sun
One tale, holding all history, is true:
The wisdom of the heart has always known
From God to God the world is passing through.

# KALI

The night of Kali falls over the world;
Ideas are without reason or rhyme.
In every passing year there is less time
And men forget the soul contains a pearl.

Who knows this moment is a gift of gold?
Who tells a story needing to be told?
Men think the circling wind of dreams is real
And they know nothing more than what they feel.

The stars that long ago were temple bells
Are quiet now; few men can hear them toll.
On earth there is a grief that will not heal
And in the heart grows something hard and cold.
The age of miracles has come and gone:
The goddess dances in the fire of dawn.

# BENARES

Today the eyes of Kali blaze,
The ego wanders in its maze;
The goddess wields her sword to cut
And by its blade the wise are taught.
Regardless of the world's wild storm,
They find God in each name and form.

To one invoking in the night
What wisdom does the Self recite?
In silence he has understood
God's closer than grain is to wood.

The life that he has left behind
Burns on a pyre deep in the mind;
And in the ashes that remain
Nothing is written but God's Name.

## SHRI LALLA

Shri Lalla's Master spoke to her one word:
*From without enter thou the inmost part.*

And so, naked, she danced into the world;
*Maya* unveiling *Atma* through her art.

Her body like the gleam of Lakshmi's glance—
The *Shakti* of the Truth must always dance.

## THE SILENCE

Dancing the beauty of the naked Truth,
Shri Lalla knew the freedom of the Real.

Hearing the melody the heart revealed—
Shri Lalla dancing with the Absolute.

Deep in the silence of the inmost Chord
Her soul dissolved like honey in the Lord.

# SANCTUARY

Closing the eyes a temple door is seen;
To enter there abandon every dream.
Where emptiness establishes its shrine
Eternity peers through its mask of time.


Deep in the sanctuary of the mind
A bell to wake a god is all we find—
When every moment is a prayer bead
The Word that silence teaches is our creed.

# THE ECHO

Invoking God, a priest of certainty
Will take the high and long view of the day.
Because he's summoned by Reality
From head to heart he travels on the way.

Around him every person says *I am*,
But few know where the echo first began.
Resounding in the cave of nothingness,
A timeless voice repeats *not this, not this*.

# THE STAR

The center of the soul is like a star;
Next to it there is nothing that is real.
Its beauty is the light of who we are
And in creation we see God revealed.

Lit from within we travel on the way;
The one thing necessary is to pray.
As we return to God we should not fear;
The star into the sunrise disappears.

# THE CHORD

A snowy mountain in a sunlit mind,
And in the body like a silent sea;
In life the flowing tide of joy we find
And in the deepest heart:  Reality.


Since Unity sings multiplicity
A man invoking God may learn a song.
Pouring himself into its melody,
He hears the chord to which all things belong.

# THE GARDEN

Invoking God, we greet the break of day;
The garden that we tend is what we pray.
With love that echoes in the good we do,
We live to learn the beautiful and true.

At dawn the birds in all their voices tell
No other wisdom than the scriptures spell.
The waking eye discerns what sages find:
Creator by creation is divined.

Eyes closed, we sow seeds of the highest art;
What blossoms but the flower of the heart?

# FLOWERS

From seeds of everlasting gratitude
There grows a garden of beatitude;
And from a soul rooted in certainty
There flows the perfume of serenity.

Beyond the suffering of every thorn
Inside a Golden Lotus we're reborn.
The spiritual eye sees deep and broad
Through every flower blooms the Face of God.

# EACH MORNING

In every age the great sages have known
God fills the world like honey in a comb.
This is the wisdom time cannot erase:
*No matter where you turn there is His Face.*

Until the moment you return to Him
Look for the Lord in every living thing.
Each morning when you rise invoke His Name
And know that Truth and Beauty are your wings.

# NO HIGHER GROUND

In every ocean wave of rising thought
God's Name is like an island in the mind.
And there surviving castaways are taught
In prayer each passing moment is defined.

Though ransoms of contingency they pay,
Arriving there they seek no higher ground.
Although some think them lost or passed away,
In solitude and silence they are found.

# THE SHELL

Because they love the Lord with all they are
Believers who have faith will go to God.
Their souls are made of joy and gratitude
And they are long absorbed in quiet prayer.

Although they go unnoticed in the world
Their words are like the sunlight and the rain.
Just as the sea inside the shell is heard,
God speaks to souls who live inside His Name.

# THE LOOM

A Unity in multiplicity;
Each bird and flower form a single strand.
The universe reflects a tapestry
And every thread is woven by God's Hand.

This carpet spreads as far as we can see;
Its weft is Peace, its warp:  Reality.
To know things deeply and to understand
The loom of God weaves wisdom into man.

# THE WHEEL

By concentration centered on the Real,
The quiet mind turns like a potter's wheel.
By virtue and discernment it is shaped—
Life is the kiln; Spirit in clay is baked.

Deeply awake inside a world of dreams,
The potter works to fashion what he means.
Each cup and pitcher will receive its due,
To pour the wine and honey of the True.

## STANDING ALONE

Standing alone, no matter where you are,
The time and place for God is here and now.
In every soul who seeks Him here-below
He is as close as light is to a star.

This moment that is now has always been.
The center of the world is where you stand.
God's closer than the sunlight on your skin;
He reaches out to hold you in His Hand.

# THE BRIDGE

# GNOSIS

The eye of certainty is like the sun—
There is no veil through which it does not see.
The center dwells in the periphery
And as each ego thinks itself alone
All numbers must contain the number one.

The depth of God is more than we can tell;
Next to the deepest knowledge of the Real
Every religion is a heresy.
Eckhart, from whom God nothing hid, knew well:
*To reach the kernel you must break the shell.*

And Ibn 'Arabi, absorbed in prayer,
Saw nothing but an ocean without shore—
Its waves are flowing still through every soul;
There is no part that does not touch the whole.

# THE QUESTION

How may we know what is beyond our sight?
Wholehearted prayer fills the world with light.
The further shore is infinitely near
And in the dawn of death the way is clear.

We say farewell to forms where shadows cling
And suffering is sown by seeds of time.
The soul in deepest silence learns to sing:
The Name of God alone makes all things rhyme.

# THE SEARCH

In search of what will make us feel complete
We think the music of desire is sweet;
But ego is the shell, and not the pearl—
And world is God, but God is not the world.

A drop of water on a lotus-leaf,
Lit by the sun this life on earth is brief.
To seek the Truth a man falls deep in thought,
While in the heart the Seeker is the Sought.

## NO FRONTIER

We bear within ourselves the saving Ark,
A rainbow in the sky reveals our way.
Because God's Name is our immortal Spark
We are the prayers we send into the day.

We read Reality with eye so clear
Our homeland is a place with no frontier.
By maps of truth and beauty we are led
Into the Realm where Seen and Seer wed.

# NO OTHER PATH

Illumined by the Name's deep glow,
The pilgrims of the dawn through darkness go.
Truth is the holy mountain they ascend;
No other path leads to their journey's end.

And while they travel, rich in poverty,
The soul grows lighter than a summer breeze—
And when they find the Real in ecstasy,
The heart's eye like a star at midnight sees.

# THE RING

The vision of the heart's eye does not fail;
All wise men see through the magician's veil.
Not moving from one place they travel far;
Like stars they need not be more than they are.

Favored by grace, abandoning all else,
Their pilgrimage leads to the deepest Self.
Like white doves flying high above the flood
All of their words are saying yes to God—

And in their souls, as every prayer takes wing,
Heaven and earth have formed a perfect ring.

## REALITY

With no vocation but Reality
The poor in God are roses on a grave.
Born in the consciousness of Unity,
Their words are shaped by gratitude and praise.

Wrapped in their robes of silence they are free
And through the vision of the heart they see
Why should they bow to gods of lesser things?
One song alone a naked traveler sings.

Why are they passing through the here-below?
To know the Truth; and be the Truth they know.

## TRAVELERS

There is a sun that rises in the dark
And by its light we see all things in God.
The Infinite sings through each finite part
And by its song the captive soul is freed.

Hearing this music, travelers take flight
And journey inward to an unknown height.
Deep in the silence of the heart they seek
The one established on the mountain peak.

## SOPHIA

She is the inward music of the Real,

And when the sages sing she is their theme.

There is no melody more beautiful;

All other songs are singing in a dream.


Seeking the knowledge time cannot erase,

Our journey finds an end in her embrace.

It's by her word we learn what life is worth

And by her touch, at death, the soul gives birth.

## THE PALACE

In consciousness of God we leave behind
The theater of *Maya* in the mind.
The here-below is weary and worn thin
And we discern the one way out leads in.

Within a Realm the pure in heart have seen
The Truth is King and Beauty is the Queen.
No other court where we will come to kneel,
No palace but the knowledge of the Real.

## IN TIME

Just as the sun shines down on all we see
The Truth must speak to all we strive to be.
For every waking heart, deep in the night,
The consciousness of God is morning light.

In time we travel through the here-below;
Each moment different, each one the same.
The road before us rises, we must go—
Our strength is found remembering God's Name.

## A FALLING STAR

A falling star across a midnight sky
Recalls the path where we are passing by.
What does not live forever fades away;
In this brief life our purpose is to pray.

To be the beauty light and love bestow
We travel where the Truth alone may go.
Within the silence of the naked soul
Remembering the One we are made whole.

## THE BRIDGE

Because there cannot be two Absolutes
The Truth is that there is no god but God.
All beauty blossoms from a sacred root
And everything we love flows from the Good.

This knowledge is a bridge to Paradise;
These words, forever new, can set us free.
Each day we rise and walk into the light
The heart knows more than what the eye can see.

## THE GOLDEN HOURS

The golden hours of Remembrance shine
And radiate an alchemy of Bliss.
In certitude we taste a sacred wine
And in serenity a waking kiss.

Each invocation like a drop of rain,
And every star repeats the Name again.
To read the doctrine written on the heart
We close our eyes and see deep in the dark

An Angel made of light stands in the soul;
He has outspread his wings to make us whole.

## THE PROMISED LAND

In consciousness of God our work is done;
Each thought leads from the many to the One.

No pilgrimage except to seek His Face;
Our journey ends as life and death embrace.

It's here and now, no matter where we stand—
Invoking God, we reach the Promised Land.

# ABOUT THE AUTHOR

Barry McDonald (1951-2021) is the author of *The Eagle's Flight* (Sophia Perennis, 2008). He is the editor of *Every Branch in Me: Essays on the Meaning of Man* (World Wisdom, 2002), *Seeing God Everywhere: Essays on Nature and the Sacred* (World Wisdom, 2003) and co-editor, with Patrick Laude, of *Music of the Sky: An Anthology of Spiritual Poetry* (World Wisdom, 2004). His writings have appeared in numerous journals in the US and abroad.

∾

Grateful acknowledgement is made to the editors of the following journals in which some of these poems first appeared: *Cross Currents: the Journal of Religion and Intellectual Life*, *Sacred Web: the Journal of Tradition and Modernity*, *Sophia: the Journal of Traditional Studies*, *Sufi Journal*, *Temenos Academy Review* and *Vincit Omnia Veritas*.

# INDEX OF FIRST LINES

Lightning Source UK Ltd.
Milton Keynes UK
UKHW010844010822
406672UK00001B/74